		DATE DUE	

Nutrition

Conquering Carbs

Kristin Petrie

ABDO
Publishing Company

visit us at
www.abdopub.com

Published by ABDO Publishing Company, 4940 Viking Drive, Edina, Minnesota 55435.
Copyright © 2004 by Abdo Consulting Group, Inc. International copyrights reserved in all
countries. No part of this book may be reproduced in any form without written permission from
the publisher.

Printed in the United States.

Cover Photo: Corbis
Interior Photos: Corbis pp. 1, 4, 7, 9, 11, 12, 13, 15, 17, 19, 21, 22, 23, 24, 26-27, 28; Corel Photo
    Disc p. 5; U.S. Department of Agriculture and U.S. Department of Health and Human
    Services p. 29

Editors: Kate A. Conley, Stephanie Hedlund, Kristianne E. Vieregger
Art Direction: Neil Klinepier

Library of Congress Cataloging-in-Publication Data

Petrie, Kristin, 1970-
    Conquering carbs / Kristin Petrie.
        p. cm. -- (Nutrition)
    Includes index.
    Summary: Discusses the different types of carbohydrates, which foods provide them, how
the body uses them, and their importance in a healthy diet.
    ISBN 1-59197-401-1
    1. Carbohydrates in human nutrition--Juvenile literature. [1. Carbohydrates. 2.
Nutrition.] I. Title.

QP701.P47 2003
613.2'83--dc21
                                                                        2002043625

Contents

Carbohydrates

Carbohydrates have had a bad reputation lately. But then again, so has fat for the past 20 years. Protein, too, was supposedly bad for you. Oh, poor **macronutrients**. Well, at least they receive some glory as eating trends and fad diets come and go.

You've probably heard people say bread and pasta are fattening. Or, maybe you have heard that sugar makes you hyper. You may also know some adults on low-carbohydrate diets.

Carbohydrate's Nickname

Sometimes people shorten the word *carbohydrate* to the word *carb*. However, both words mean the exact same thing.

Pasta is one of hundreds of foods that are rich in carbs.

On the other hand, some people say you should eat lots of carbohydrates. In fact, carbohydrates are the base of the **Food Guide Pyramid**. Yes, all of this conflicting information is very confusing.

But keep reading, and the importance of carbohydrates will become clear. Our knowledge of **nutrition** will never stop changing. However, studies show that people who eat nutritious, carbohydrate-rich foods appear healthier than those who make other **nutrients** the base of their diets.

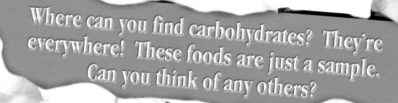

Carbohydrate-Rich Foods

Where can you find carbohydrates? They're everywhere! These foods are just a sample. Can you think of any others?

bread   milk   bananas   rice   cookies   potatoes
apples   cereal   yogurt   corn   noodles   popcorn

Different Carbs

Now that we can picture some carbohydrate-rich foods, let's take a microscope and look deeper into them. Carbohydrates come in three different forms. They are sugar, starch, and fiber. No matter what their structure, all carbohydrates are made of the same **elements**. They are carbon, hydrogen, and oxygen.

Sugars are called simple carbohydrates or simple sugars. Starches and fiber are called complex carbohydrates. The difference between simple and complex carbohydrates is their chemical structure.

Simple sugars are made of one or just a few sugar units in a simple chain. Starches and fiber are made of many sugar units in chains that twist and turn like crazy jungle gyms.

What Does the Word *Carbohydrate* Mean?

The word *carbohydrate* is a combination of the names for carbon, hydrogen, and oxygen. *Carbo* means carbon. *Hydrate* means water. Water is formed from the combination of hydrogen and oxygen.

Opposite page: An apple has both simple and complex carbohydrates.

Simple Carbs

Simple carbohydrates are usually sweet tasting. Foods made with white sugar, such as cookies, candy, soda, and fruit drinks, are examples. Some foods from nature, such as honey and fruits, are also sources of simple carbohydrates.

Monosaccharides are the simplest form of carbohydrates. They contain just one cluster of the **elements** carbon, hydrogen, and oxygen. Glucose is the most commonly known monosaccharide.

Disaccharides are two carbon, hydrogen, and oxygen clusters that are joined together. Sucrose is a disaccharide that forms when two monosaccharides are joined. Lactose is another disaccharide you may be familiar with. It is the sugar naturally found in milk.

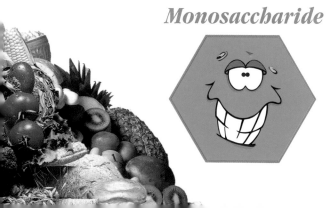

Monosaccharide   *Disaccharide*

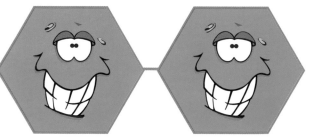

Cookies are a great example of a simple sugar treat.

The Jobs of a Simple Carb

Monosaccharides, such as glucose, don't have to be **digested**. They enter your bloodstream and begin to circulate almost immediately. Disaccharides are digested quickly and then they, too, enter the bloodstream.

For these reasons, energy from simple carbohydrates is used up nearly as fast as it is produced. So, they are good for times when you need quick bursts of energy.

Simple carbohydrates have other functions as well. Sugars are usually appreciated for their sweet taste. They also add pleasant smells, textures, and colors to foods. Sugars make certain foods, such as cookies, crispy. They make other foods, such as fudge, creamy. Sugars also help develop the brown crust on the top of baked goods, such as cakes and muffins.

Quick Energy

Can you think of a time when you needed a quick burst of energy? How about when you are sprinting to catch the bus or riding your bike up a hill?

Opposite page: Junk food is only bad for you when you eat too much of it or when it replaces healthier food in your diet.

Simple Sugars

Eat your cake and be healthy, too! Sugar, in moderation, can be part of a well-balanced diet. Sugar gives you energy and makes food look, feel, and taste delicious. But, like anything else, too much is not a good idea.

Simple sugar is not harmful to your body. It doesn't make you hyper or cause **diabetes**. It isn't addictive, and it won't make you fat—unless you eat too much.

As a result, sugary foods can have a healthy place in your diet. Sugary foods, however, should never replace foods that provide your body with **nutrients**. That's because there are few **vitamins** and **minerals** in many simple-sugar foods.

Whole grain foods are healthier for you because they generally have more nutrients.

Moderation is the key to a healthy diet.

Complex Carbs

When we think of carbohydrates, starchy foods such as bread, potatoes, pasta, and rice are often the first to come to mind. These are good examples of foods rich in complex carbohydrates.

Complex carbohydrates are longer chains of the same sugar units that make up simple carbohydrates. So, if they are made of the same carbon and water clusters, why don't starches such as rice and bread taste sweet?

The bigger **molecules** that make up a starchy food's structure do not fit on your tongue's taste buds! If you want to get a sweeter taste from a starchy food, you can chew it and keep it in your mouth longer. This lets **enzymes** in your mouth break down the starchy food.

Eventually, the starchy food breaks down into smaller and smaller sugar units. These smaller molecules fit onto your taste buds, giving the food a sweet taste.

Polysaccharides

Complex carbohydrates have a scientific name. They are called polysaccharides. *Poly* means many, and *saccharide* means sugar. Put them together, and you have many sugars.

Complex carbs help you stay focused because they keep you feeling full for a long time.

The Jobs of a Complex Carb

The longer chains of **molecules** in complex carbohydrates give foods different tastes. Thank goodness for that, because sweet food all the time would become very boring!

In addition, the longer chains in complex carbohydrates take more time to **digest**. So, your body needs more time before it can release these carbohydrates into your blood as glucose. For this reason, complex carbohydrates give you energy more slowly.

Complex carbohydrates also help your energy level last through the fourth quarter or the ninth inning! Foods that are high in complex carbohydrates also provide lots of the **vitamins** and **minerals** your body needs.

Opposite page: Most cereals are packed with nutrients, including complex carbohydrates.

Fiber

Fiber is another complex carbohydrate that is important to your health. Fiber does not taste sweet. But, it adds texture to food and makes you feel full. The body does not **digest** all parts of fiber's chemical structure, and this is good for your health. There are two types of dietary fiber, **insoluble** and **soluble**. They each have distinct roles.

Insoluble fiber travels through your digestive system pretty much unchanged. In your large intestine it acts like a sponge, absorbing water and adding bulk. This process keeps waste products moving quickly.

Soluble fiber helps keep down the amount of **cholesterol** in your blood. It also helps your blood glucose level stay even. These functions of soluble fiber may protect you from heart disease and **diabetes**.

How Much Fiber?

You can figure out how much fiber to eat by adding the number five to your age. The sum is how many grams of fiber you need each day. For example, if you are seven years old, you need to eat 12 grams of fiber every day.

Many cereals, such as raisin bran or oatmeal, and whole wheat bread are great sources of fiber. They also have other complex carbohydrates, **vitamins**, and **minerals**. Add some fresh fruit such as strawberries or blueberries to your cereal, and you're set!

Whole grain breads are full of healthy fiber.

Nutrition

Of course, all carbohydrates are not equal when it comes to your health. Whole grain breads and cereals, rice, beans, pasta, vegetables, and fruits are considered **nutrient** dense. They are high in carbohydrates, as well as **vitamins**, **minerals**, and protein.

In fact, there is even a difference between the **nutritional** values of different carbohydrate-rich foods. Whole wheat or whole grain products are made with flour containing the entire grain. White flour, on the other hand, has had many of the great nutrients removed in order to make it smooth.

You can taste the difference between these types of foods. For example, whole wheat bread tastes grainier than white bread. It even takes longer to chew and swallow. However, foods made with more processed ingredients are smoother and faster to chew and swallow.

Some foods are made with highly refined flour and a lot of simple sugars. You may think of these as sweets. Cake, candy, and cookies are often called empty calories, because they contain very few **nutrients**. To receive the most **nutritional** value, start with nutrient-dense breads and pastas, as well as fruits and vegetables.

Apples make a great snack. They are packed with fiber, vitamins, and minerals.

Digestion

Carbohydrates must be broken down into their simplest form before your body can absorb and use them. The difference between simple and complex carbohydrates is the amount of time it takes to reach the same form.

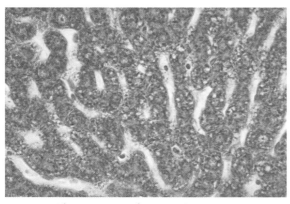

Glycogen under a microscope

When you eat a carbohydrate, **enzymes** in your mouth start working. Enzymes continue to work all the way through your **digestive** system. They break down the carbohydrates into the smallest sugar clusters possible.

Once your food is digested, glucose begins to travel in your blood. Glucose is the most common form of carbohydrate used in your body. You may also have heard it called blood sugar. Glucose causes your blood sugar level to rise until it has been absorbed into cells and tissues.

Once absorbed, glucose gives your entire body energy. Other glucose is stored in your liver and muscles. It is called glycogen and is used when your diet doesn't provide enough carbohydrates. Excess glucose is converted to body fat.

Take your time when you are eating. This will make digestion easier for your body.

Gluconeogenesis

Your brain, muscles, and other organs need glucose to function. Because of its importance, the body has two amazing backup plans for making glucose. First, the body stores glucose as glycogen. Second, an amazing process called gluconeogenesis can make glucose.

Eating balanced meals will help prevent your body from breaking down important muscles for energy.

Gluconeogenesis begins when your glycogen stores are gone and your diet does not provide enough carbohydrates. In this process, your body uses the proteins that make up your muscles and organs to make glucose.

Losing muscles and breaking down other vital organs to provide glucose, as you can imagine, is not ideal. Gluconeogenesis exists only to provide glucose when you do not or cannot feed yourself properly. So, eat your carbohydrates!

Energy for Exercising

When you exercise, your body releases stored energy from either glycogen or fat. If you are sprinting or doing another quick exercise, your body calls on blood glucose and glycogen for energy. If you are exercising for a long time, however, your body uses fat for energy.

Gluconeogenesis

What does the word gluconeogenesis mean? It's easy to figure out if you break down the word into smaller parts. *Gluco* means glucose. *Neo* means new. *Genesis* means create. Put them together and you have formed a word that means creating new glucose!

Carb Contributions

Hunger, even just from missing breakfast, makes it difficult to think. Giving your body carbohydrate-rich fuel at breakfast will help you be more alert and do better at school. Eating breakfast also helps you be more creative and energetic. Being alert, creative, and energetic—rather than tired and cranky—will certainly affect your desire to be at school.

Breakfast is the most important meal of the day. It is the first food your body has had in several hours.

Without breakfast, it is hard to get enough of the **nutrients** you need to grow, learn, play, and stay healthy. Any traditional or wacky breakfast will do. Try cereal or toast, milk and a fruit kabob, a slice of pizza, or even a taco! All of these will give you energy.

A **nutritious** breakfast also gives you protein, **vitamins**, and **minerals**. Look for **enriched** breakfast cereals—they really pack a punch when it comes to getting the good stuff. People who skip breakfast are unlikely to receive enough nutrients and calories by the end of the day.

The Benefits of Breakfast

Breakfast is a good time to catch up with your family. Or, eating at school is a good time to catch up with friends. Either way, sitting down to eat with others is important for your mind and your body.

Test It Out!

What would your day be like without some quick energy to get you going? You'd be draggin'! Test it out!

One weekend morning, eat a breakfast of an egg and sausage or other meat. Remember, no pancakes, toast, orange juice, fruit, or milk because they are all carbohydrate rich! Write down what you ate, and how you feel just after eating, as well as an hour or so later. Do you have energy? Feel happy? Blah?

The next day, eat a balanced breakfast, such as a bowl of cereal or pancakes, and some fruit or juice. Again, write down what you ate and how you feel. From this unscientific test, you may see differences in how your body feels depending on if you eat carbohydrate-rich foods.

A healthy breakfast includes a combination of all nutrients.

After completing this carb test, you may wonder how many carbs you should eat daily. Look to the **Food Guide Pyramid** to determine this. Remember that it is most important to know where the most **nutrients** come from in each food group. Eating a variety of nutrient-dense foods instead of empty calories will help you feel your best. It will also help your body grow and stay healthy.

The Food Guide Pyramid

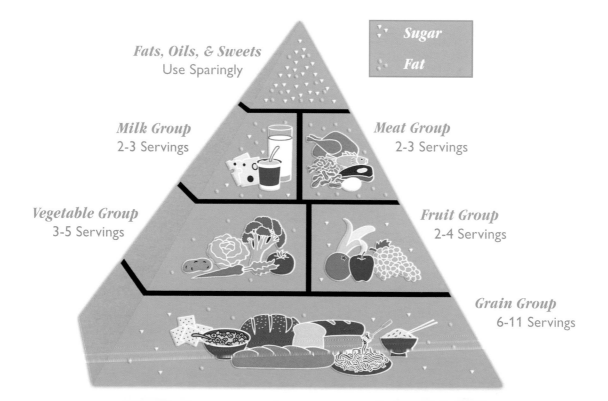

Glossary

cholesterol - a type of fat that can clog blood vessels.

diabetes - a disease in which a person's body cannot properly absorb normal amounts of sugar and starch.

digestion - to break down food into substances small enough for the body to absorb.

element - one of more than 100 basic substances from which all other things are made.

enriched - foods that have had nutrients added to replace those lost in food processing.

enzyme - a complex protein produced in the living cells of all plants and animals. It is used in many of the body's functions, from digestion to clotting.

Food Guide Pyramid - a chart used to describe dietary guidelines for Americans.

insoluble - won't dissolve in a substance such as water.

macronutrients - the largest nutrients found in food. They include carbohydrates, proteins, fats, and water.

mineral - a tiny, inorganic molecule that does not give energy but is needed in small amounts by the body.

molecule - the smallest piece of a substance that is still the same substance. A molecule breaks down into one or more atoms.

nutrient - a substance found in food and used in the body to promote growth, maintenance, and repair.

nutrition - the study of nutrients and the processes of eating, digesting, absorbing, transporting, using, storing, and excreting these substances.

soluble - dissolves in a substance such as water.

vitamin - a tiny, organic molecule that does not give energy but is needed in small amounts by the body.

Saying It

carbohydrate - kahr-boh-HI-drayt
cholesterol - kuh-LES-tuh-rohl
disaccharide - di-SA-kuh-ride
enzyme - EN-zime
gluconeogenesis - gloo-kuh-nee-uh-JEH-nuh-suhs
glucose - GLOO-kohs
glycogen - GLI-kuh-juhn

insoluble - in-SAHL-yuh-buhl
lactose - LAK-tohs
macronutrient - MA-kroh-NOO-tree-uhnt
monosaccharide - mah-nuh-SA-kuh-ride
soluble - SAHL-yuh-buhl
sucrose - SOO-krohs

Web Sites

To learn more about carbohydrates, visit ABDO Publishing Company on the World Wide Web at **www.abdopub.com**. Web sites about nutrition are featured on our Book Links page. These links are routinely monitored and updated to provide the most current information available.

Index